Put Beginning Readers on the Right Track with
ALL ABOARD READING™

The All Aboard Reading series is especially for beginning readers. Written by noted authors and illustrated in full color, these are books that children really and truly *want* to read—books to excite their imagination, tickle their funny bone, expand their interests, and support their feelings. With four different reading levels, All Aboard Reading lets you choose which books are most appropriate for your children and their growing abilities.

Picture Readers—for Ages 3 to 6
Picture Readers have super-simple texts, with many nouns appearing as rebus pictures. At the end of each book are 24 flash cards—on one side is the rebus picture; on the other side is the written-out word.

Level 1—for Preschool through First-Grade Children
Level 1 books have very few lines per page, very large type, easy words, lots of repetition, and pictures with visual "cues" to help children figure out the words on the page.

Level 2—for First-Grade to Third-Grade Children
Level 2 books are printed in slightly smaller type than Level 1 books. The stories are more complex, but there is still lots of repetition in the text, and many pictures. The sentences are quite simple and are broken up into short lines to make reading easier.

Level 3—for Second-Grade through Third-Grade Children
Level 3 books have considerably longer texts, harder words, and more complicated sentences.

All Aboard for happy reading!

To my husband Jay Clarke
for loving and supporting me,
to my friend and mentor Tanya Dean
for training and encouraging me,
and to my parents Karen Hamilton and Roy Norris
for giving me a love of reading—G.L.C.

To Melissa, my agent, my confidante—N.T.

Text copyright © 2000 by Ginjer L. Clarke. Illustrations copyright © 2000 by Neecy Twinem.
All rights reserved. Published by Grosset & Dunlap, a division of Penguin Putnam Books
for Young Readers, New York. ALL ABOARD READING is a trademark of The Putnam &
Grosset Group. GROSSET & DUNLAP is a trademark of Grosset & Dunlap, Inc. Published
simultaneously in Canada. Printed in the U.S.A.

Library of Congress Cataloging-in-Publication Data is available.

ISBN 0-448-41851-7 (GB)   A B C D E F G H I J
ISBN 0-448-42095-3 (pb)   A B C D E F G H I J

ALL
ABOARD
READING™

Level 2
Grades 1-3

Baby ALLIGATOR

By Ginjer L. Clarke
Illustrated by Neecy Twinem

Grosset & Dunlap • New York

It is morning on a lake in Florida.

A baby animal is crying.

Cheep! Cheep! Cheep!

It sounds like a bird.

But is it?

No!

It is a baby alligator in a nest

of sticks and leaves and mud.

She has cut open her soft egg.

She pokes out her head.

She blinks her big, black eyes.

All around her,
other baby alligators break out
of their shells, too.
It is a big family.
As many as forty babies
are born at one time—
all from the same mother!

The baby alligator is

only about nine inches long.

She is black with pale yellow stripes.

Later, her stripes will fade away.

She has bony plates on her back.

Her legs, sides, and belly are covered

with smooth, horny scales.

The little alligator
is very hungry.
She begins to wiggle
toward the water.

12

The mother alligator takes
some of the babies
to the lake.
She carries them
in her mouth.

It is not a long trip.

But danger is all around.

Otters, raccoons, snakes,

and birds are nearby.

They like to eat

baby alligators.

The little alligator is lucky.

She makes it to the water.

Now she can eat lots of

insects, snails, tadpoles, and fish.

In about six years,

when she is a big alligator,

she will eat raccoons,

snakes, birds, and turtles.

What about people?

Do alligators eat them?

Most people are too big

for alligators to eat.

But alligators are

not friendly animals.

The baby's mouth is full of sharp teeth.

When she loses a tooth,

another will grow back

in its place right away.

She may have as many as

six thousand teeth in her lifetime!

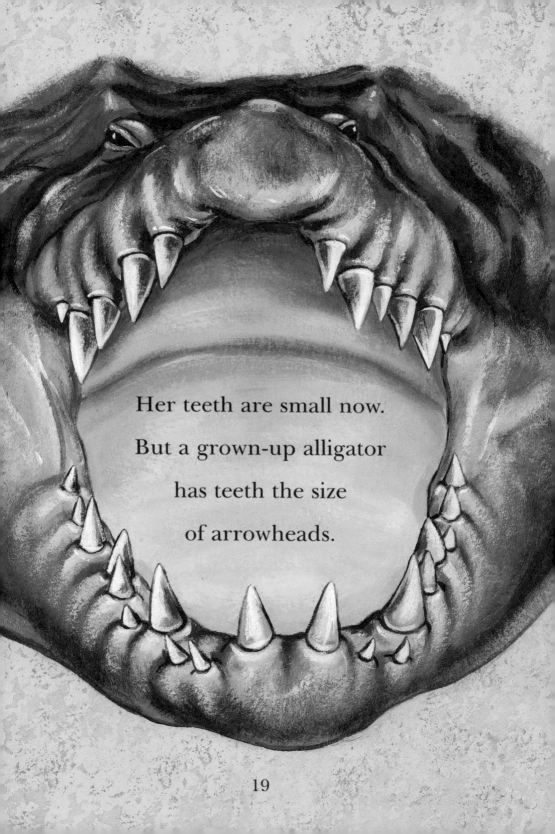

Her teeth are small now.
But a grown-up alligator
has teeth the size
of arrowheads.

Male alligators can grow

to be 15 feet long.

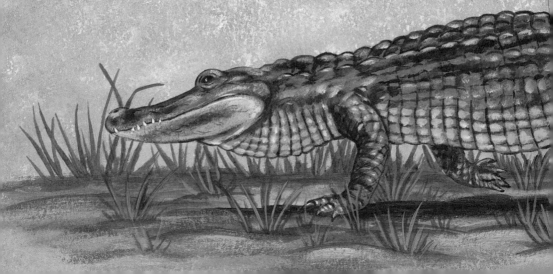

That is as long as

a pickup truck!

Now the little alligator

is six months old.

She is one foot long.

She is a good swimmer.

She can wave her tail

back and forth.

She also has webbed feet,

like a duck.

The little alligator can stay
underwater for a long time.
She can close her throat,
nose, and ears.
No water can get inside.

She also can see in the dark
like a cat.
At night, the little alligator
hunts for food.

She hides from animals
until they get close—
then she snaps them up!

Many months have passed.

Winter is coming.

Soon it will be too cold

for her to stay outside.

So she digs a deep tunnel in the mud.

She will stay there until spring.

Alligators are
cold-blooded animals.
That means that their body
temperature changes as the
temperature outside changes.
Hot weather makes
their temperature go up.
Cold weather makes
their temperature go down.
People are
warm-blooded animals.
Unless you have a fever,
your body temperature
stays the same.

Alligators are reptiles.

They have scaly skin like snakes

and long tails like lizards.

The word alligator

comes from the Spanish word

for lizard—el lagarto.

All reptiles are cold-blooded.

Crocodiles are reptiles, too.

They look a lot like alligators.

But when a crocodile shuts its mouth,

you can still see the big front teeth.

This is called a "crocodile smile."

Crocodiles live in many places

in the world.

Alligators live only in two places—

the southern United States and China.

Alligators and crocodiles

have been around

since the time of dinosaurs.

Scientists have found

the bones of a crocodile

called <u>Deinosuchus</u>.

(You say it like this: dy-no-SUCK-es.)

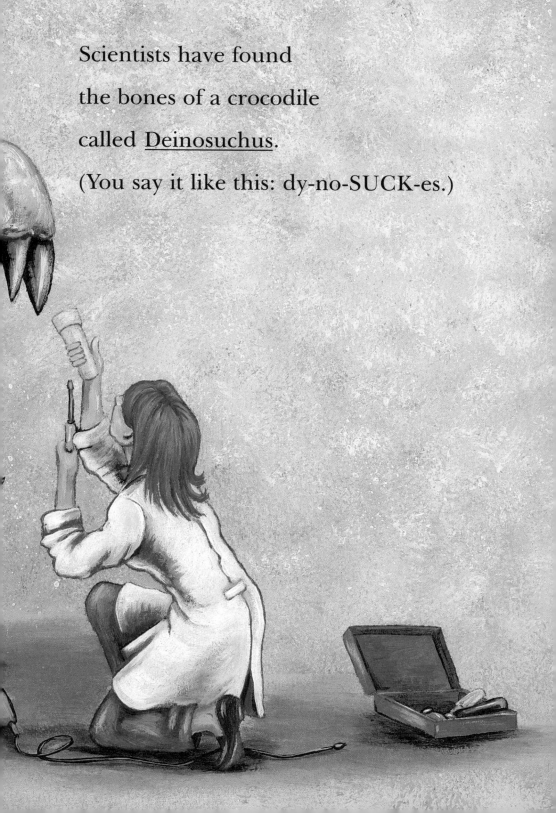

Deinosuchus was

45 feet long!

Its jaws were huge.

It had teeth like daggers.

It may have hunted dinosaurs.

Not very long ago,

hunters were free to kill alligators.

Purses and shoes were made
from their shiny, smooth skins.
Now alligators are protected
by laws in most places.
But people still kill alligators
because they are afraid of them.

Maybe now that you know
more about alligators,
you will not be too afraid of them.
Just be very careful.